My Doggie Best Friend, Z

Angelo Mariano

illustrated by Kelsey Marshalsey

This book is dedicated to my granddaughter, Ripples.
Her spunky personality and curious nature
were my inspiration for this story.

Paperback ISBN: 978-1-990336-52-2
Hardcover ISBN: 978-1-990336-53-9

Contact the publisher for Library and Archives Canada
catalogue information.

℥R

ALANNA RUSNAK PUBLISHING
Alanna Rusnak Publishing is an imprint of Chicken House Press
chickenhousepress.ca

My name is Ripples.

This is Z,
my big doggie sister.
She is 8 years old.

Z is a whippet.
My mommy and daddy brought
Z home when she was a puppy.

Ripples

Z

Z loves to cuddle with me,
my daddy, and my mommy.
We cuddle all the time.

Z always puts her head on me
when we cuddle. I think she
feels that it keeps me safe.

Z is always so excited
when we go for walks.

She jumps up as soon as she
hears the jingle of her leash.

On our walks, Z loves to see
all her doggie friends.

jingle ♪ ♫ ♪

jingle ♪ ♫

Charlie is Z's
best doggie friend.

Charlie is a
King Charles black coat;
he is a lot older than Z.

He's like a grandpa doggie.

Charlie

Z and Charlie could play
all day long.

Charlie loves to eat sticks.
He taught Z how to eat sticks.
They like to eat sticks
together.

My daddy takes the sticks
away from her, but she keeps
finding new ones.

Z's other doggie friend
on our street is Rose.

Rose is a Black Greyhound.

Rose is skinny, just like Z.

They can both run so fast.

They chase each other all
around the doggie park until
they are both so tired.

I share all my treats with Z.
She really likes my treats.

I drop them off my plate
on purpose for her to eat.

My mommy and daddy don't like it
when I do that, but Z really does.

She also really likes her doggie treats.

She loves crunchy treats the most.

Z lets me climb up on to her.

She helped me
when I started to walk.

I would sometimes hang
on to her so I could stand up.

I know that she does not really like it
when I do that, but she still lets me!

Z sometimes licks me on my face.

She knows that I don't really like it,
but I let her anyway.

I know that she does it
because she loves me!

We take Z everywhere we go.

She loves to visit my Grandpas
and my Grandmas.

They are always so happy to see her.

My Grandpa Angus has
a doggie named Dora.

Dora is a rescue doggie
from the Dominican Republic
and she is 10 years old.

Grandpa adopted her when she was 4.

Dora does not really like other dogs,
but she really likes Z. I think she feels
like she is Z's big sister.

My Grandpa Angus and I like
watching Z and Dora play together.

Grandma Tatiana has a doggie too.

His name is Max and he is a Cockapoo.

Max is a really old doggie.
He also looks like a grandpa doggie.

Max is a little bit grumpy with Z,
but Z does not mind.

Even though Max is grumpy,
Z still really likes to go over to
Grandma's and spend time with
Grandma Tatiana and Auntie Megan.

My Grandpa Pierre
and Grandma Frida
have a big yard.

They love it when Z and I go to visit
so they can play with us in the yard.

Grandpa Pierre and Grandma Frida
throw Z's ball really far
so that Z can go and fetch it.

I don't throw the ball far, but I think
Z still has fun chasing it anyway!

After a long day playing,
Z likes to lie down on the couch and nap.

I also have naps during the day,
but I do not like them.

I would rather play.

Z always seems to know
when I am not feeling so good.

She stays close to me all day
when I am sick.

She lies down beside me
and keeps me warm.

I love Z so much.

Z is my best friend in the whole world
and I think that I'm her best person
friend in the whole world.

Z is always by my side, even at nighttime!

She puts her head on me and we fall
asleep together on her doggie bed.

THE END

www.ingramcontent.com/pod-product-compliance
Lightning Source LLC
Chambersburg PA
CBHW042126040426
42450CB00002B/81